Fact Finders®

EXPLORING HISTORY THROUGH FOOD

CIVIL WAR COOKING: THE UNION

by Susan Dosier

CAPSTONE PRESS
a capstone imprint

Fact Finder Books are published by Capstone Press,
1710 Roe Crest Drive, North Mankato, Minnesota 56003.
www.mycapstonepub.com

Library of Congress Cataloging-in-Publication Data
Names: Dosier, Susan, author.
Title: Civil War cooking: the Union / by Susan Dosier.
Description: North Mankato, Minnesota: Capstone Press, [2017] |
Series: Fact finders. Exploring history through food. | Audience: Ages 9–12. |
   Audience: Grades 4–6. | Includes bibliographical references and index.
Identifiers: LCCN 2015051230 | ISBN 9781515723530 (library binding) |
   ISBN 9781515723578 (ebook pdf)
Subjects: LCSH: Cooking, American—History—Juvenile literature. | United
   States—History—Civil War, 1861–1865—Juvenile literature. | Food
   habits—United States—History—19th century—Juvenile literature. | LCGFT: Cookbooks.
Classification: LCC TX715 .D68745 2017 | DDC 641.5973/09034—dc23
LC record available at http://lccn.loc.gov/2015051230

Editorial Credits
Editor: Nikki Potts
Designer: Kayla Rossow
Media Researcher: Jo Miller
Production Specialist: Steve Walker

Photo Credits
Alamy: The Protected Art Archive, 11; Capstone Studio: Karon Dubke, back cover (fried apples,
navy bean soup), 1 (soup and fried apples), 21, 23; Corbis: Bettmann/Mathew B. Brady, cover (inset);
Getty Images: Buyenlarge, 12; Library of Congress, 8, 9; Shutterstock: Alexeysun, 15 (rolling pin),
bonchan, 1 (stew), 17, Cheryl E. Davis, 15, Dimedrol68, 14, 20, Everett Historical, 6, Glenn Price,
1 (johnnycakes), 19, Jennifer Sharp, 26, Joshua Resnick, back cover (mac and cheese), 25, Monkey
Business Images, 28, Tischenko Irina, cover (apples and background)

Design Elements
Shutterstock: 4Max, Amawasri Pakdara, Mliberra, Vitaly Korovin

Printed and bound in the USA
009670CGF16

TABLE OF CONTENTS

Chapter 1
The Civil War 6

Chapter 2
Feeding the Soldiers 10

Chapter 3
Foraging for Survival 12

Chapter 4
Making the Most of Meat 16

Chapter 5
Breads and Soups 18

Chapter 6
Dried and Fresh Fruits...........22

Chapter 7
Life Back Home..................24

Chapter 8
The Union at Christmas..........26

Recipes

Cherry Cobbler.....................14
Irish Stew.........................17
Johnnycake........................19
Navy Bean Soup....................20
Skillet-fried Apples................23
Macaroni and Cheese 25
Tea Cake Cookies..................27
Gingerbread 29

Cooking Help

Kitchen Safety 4
Metric Conversion 4
Cooking Equipment.................5

References

Glossary..........................30
Read More.........................31
Internet Sites 31
Index 32

KITCHEN SAFETY

1. Make sure your hair and clothes will not be in the way while you are cooking.
2. Keep a fire extinguisher in the kitchen. Never put water on a grease fire.
3. Wash your hands with soap before you start to cook. Wash your hands with soap again after you handle meat or poultry.
4. Ask an adult for help with sharp knives, the stove, the oven, and all electrical appliances.
5. Turn handles of pots and pans to the middle of the stove. A person walking by could run into handles that stick out toward the room.
6. Use pot holders to take dishes out of the oven.
7. Wash all fruits and vegetables.
8. Always use a clean cutting board. Wash the cutting board thoroughly after cutting meat or poultry.
9. Wipe up spills immediately.
10. Store leftovers properly. Do not leave leftovers out at room temperature for more than two hours.

METRIC CONVERSION

U.S.	Canada	U.S.	Canada	Fahrenheit	Celsius
1 quart	1 liter	1/4 teaspoon	1 mL	325 degrees	160 degrees
1 ounce	30 grams	1/2 teaspoon	2 mL	350 degrees	180 degrees
2 ounces	55 grams	1 teaspoon	5 mL	375 degrees	190 degrees
4 ounces	85 gram	1 tablespoon	15 mL	400 degrees	200 degrees
1/2 pound	225 grams	1/4 cup	50 mL	425 degrees	220 degrees
1 pound	455 grams	1/3 cup	75 m		
		1/2 cup	125 mL		
		2/3 cup	150 mL		
		3/4 cup	175 mL		
		1 cup	250 mL		

COOKING EQUIPMENT

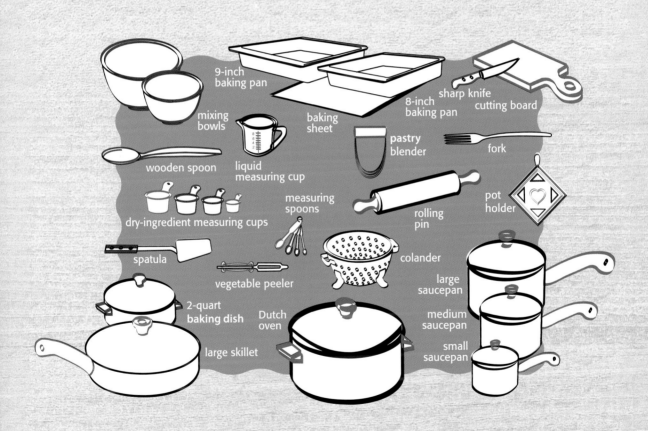

9-inch baking pan

mixing bowls

baking sheet

8-inch baking pan

sharp knife

cutting board

wooden spoon

liquid measuring cup

pastry blender

fork

dry-ingredient measuring cups

measuring spoons

rolling pin

pot holder

spatula

vegetable peeler

colander

large saucepan

2-quart baking dish

Dutch oven

medium saucepan

large skillet

small saucepan

CHAPTER 1

THE CIVIL WAR

In 1860 economic differences divided the northern and the southern United States. Some people in the North worked on small farms. But many people owned businesses or worked in factories. Many Southerners made their living by growing cotton on **plantations**. Plantation owners depended on slaves to do this work. Slave traders captured West Africans and brought them to North America. These West African slaves were bought and sold as property. Northerners and Southerners disagreed about the issue of slavery.

African-American slaves worked from sunrise to sunset in the cotton fields.

plantation—large farm found in warm areas; before the Civil War, plantations in the South used slave labor

Abraham Lincoln won the presidential election in 1860. He was a member of the Republican Party and was against slavery. Many Southerners disagreed with Lincoln's political views. They began to talk about their states leaving the United States. South Carolina declared that the federal government had unlawfully taken over rights reserved for the states. South Carolina became the first southern state to secede from the Union. Ten other southern states also left the Union within a year. These 11 states formed their own country, which they called the Confederate States of America.

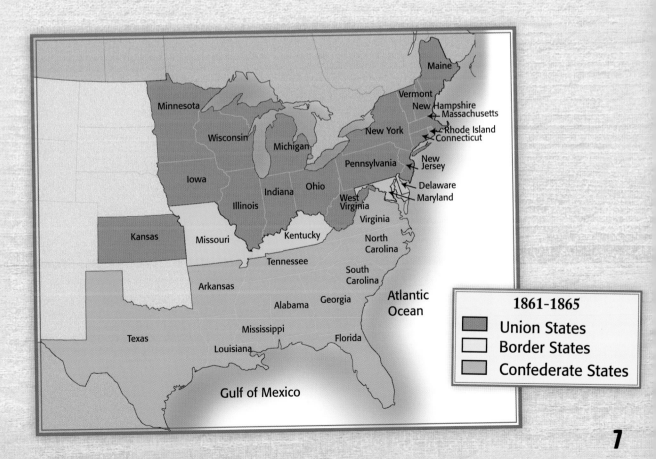

In April 1861 U.S. soldiers serving at Fort Sumter were running out of supplies. Fort Sumter was located in South Carolina. Southerners believed the fort belonged to the Confederacy. They hoped the Union soldiers would leave the fort when they faced starvation. Instead President Lincoln ordered federal ships to bring food and supplies to the Union troops at Fort Sumter. This action was the trigger for the Civil War (1861–1865).

Union soldiers were called Yankees. Confederate soldiers were called Rebels. Yankees wore blue uniforms and Rebels wore gray uniforms. The fighting continued for four long years. The Confederacy **surrendered** to the Union Army on April 9, 1865. The Union victory also put an end to slavery.

Southerners fire upon the soldiers serving at Fort Sumter in South Carolina.

surrender—to give up, or admit defeat in a fight or battle

Soldiers fill up their water canteens at their camp in Fredericksburg, Virginia.

WATER

A Civil War soldier needed water for many reasons: to drink, to make coffee or tea, to prepare and boil food, and to wash. But clean water was not always easy to find. Soldiers carried water in **canteens** and refilled them from wells. Soldiers also drew water from rivers, lakes, ponds, or even puddles. When only muddy or dirty water was available, soldiers strained it through an old shirt or handkerchief before drinking it.

canteen—a small metal container for holding water

CHAPTER 2

FEEDING THE SOLDIERS

The Union Army was better able to feed its soldiers than the Confederate Army. The Union had more money and could afford to buy more food for each soldier. Because few battles were fought in the North, many of the Union's supply lines were not damaged. The open **routes** allowed suppliers to regularly reach the Union Army.

Although Yankees had more food than Rebels did, Union soldiers sometimes went hungry. One soldier wrote, "Some days we live first rate, and then the next, we don't have half enough." Soldiers called the supply lines "cracker lines." This name may have come about because supply lines, like crisp crackers, often broke down before food could reach the men.

route—the road or course followed to get somewhere

COOKING

Union soldiers who lived in permanent camps or **barracks** did not cook for themselves. Army cooks prepared meals for the soldiers. Union soldiers who were on long marches or were fighting in battles had to do their own cooking.

Whether they lived in barracks or on the battlefield, soldiers were divided into messes. Messes were groups of four to eight men. These men ate their meals together. The soldiers also cooked together if they were marching. They sometimes took turns cooking. The soldier who could cook the best often made all the meals. A mess occasionally hired a free black man to cook for them.

an officer mess in Bealeton, Virginia

barracks—the part of a fort where soldiers sleep

CHAPTER 3

FORAGING FOR SURVIVAL

When rations were low, soldiers often **foraged** for food in nearby woods. Blackberries, honey, wild cherries, apples, grapes, **persimmons**, and other fruits often were plentiful in summer months. Union Army regulations did not allow soldiers to steal food. But officers often overlooked this rule. Foraging became necessary when soldiers were starving and needed food to survive.

A foraging party returns with food for the Union Army at Annandale Chapel, Virginia, 1861.

forage—to search for food
persimmon—an orange-red fruit that is shaped like a plum and is sweet and soft when ripe

UNION RATIONS

According to ration lists, the Union Army appeared to have the best-fed soldiers in the world. But the men did not get their full **ration** of food every day. Depending on the season, food sometimes was plentiful. Other times food was scarce.

The following list shows the daily amounts of food rationed to Union soldiers from August 3, 1861, to June 20, 1864.

To each soldier:
12 ounces of pork or bacon or 1 pound and
    4 ounces of salt beef or fresh beef
1 pound and 6 ounces of soft bread or flour
    or 1 pound of hard bread or 1 pound and
    4 ounces of **cornmeal**

For every 100 soldiers:
15 pounds of beans or peas
10 pounds of rice or hominy
10 pounds of green coffee or 8 pounds
    of roasted coffee beans or 1 pound
    and 8 ounces of tea
15 pounds of sugar
4 quarts of vinegar
3 pounds and 12 ounces of salt
4 ounces of pepper
30 pounds of potatoes
1 quart of molasses

ration—a soldier's daily share of food
cornmeal—corn that is coarsely ground

13

CHERRY COBBLER

Soldiers sometimes made fruit cobblers or pies after a successful forage in the countryside. They baked the cobbler in a covered pot in a bed of coals. The crusts of these desserts often were tough. But cobblers were still a treat.

INGREDIENTS

2 (16-ounce) cans tart red
   cherries, drained
1 cup sugar
2 tablespoons cornstarch
1/4 teaspoon ground cinnamon
1-1/2 cups all-purpose flour
1 tablespoon butter for greasing
3/4 teaspoon salt
1/2 cup shortening
5 tablespoons cold water

EQUIPMENT

medium saucepan
dry-ingredient measuring cups
measuring spoons
wooden spoon
8-inch by 8-inch (20-centimeter by
   20-cm) baking pan
large mixing bowl
fork or pastry blender
paper towel or napkin
   for greasing
rolling pin
knife
cutting board

Ask an adult to help you prepare this recipe.

1. Combine cherries, 1 cup sugar, and 2 tablespoons cornstarch in saucepan. Let stand 10 minutes.

2. Cook over medium heat, stirring constantly, until thickened and bubbly.

3. Stir in 1/4 teaspoon cinnamon.

4. Grease baking pan with 1 tablespoon butter and paper towel or napkin. Pour mixture into dish. Cool slightly.

5. Mix 1-1/2 cups flour and 3/4 teaspoon salt in bowl.

6. Cut in 1/2 cup shortening with a fork or pastry blender until mixture is in small clumps.

7. Add 5 tablespoons cold water, 1 tablespoon at a time, stirring with a fork until mixture forms a ball.

8. Heat oven to 375°F (190°C).

9. Lightly flour cutting board.

10. Pat dough into a circle on floured cutting board.

11. Roll dough to 1/8-inch (3-millimeter) thickness.

12. Cut dough into 1/2-inch-wide (12-mm-wide) strips.

13. Lay strips criss-cross over cherry mixture.

14. Bake 40 minutes, until crust strips are lightly browned.

Makes 6 servings.

CHAPTER 4

MAKING THE MOST OF MEAT

Meat was the most common source of **protein** for Union soldiers. Usually fresh beef was not part of their rations. Supply wagons had no way of keeping the meat cold until it reached the soldiers. Rations usually included pickled beef because it did not spoil as quickly as fresh meat.

Pork was probably the most common type of meat rationed to Union soldiers. Smoked ham and bacon did not spoil as quickly, and the high fat content of pork provided soldiers with lard. They fried cornmeal, potatoes, and other foods in lard.

Fish and wild game such as possum and squirrel provided protein for soldiers when other meat was scarce. Chicken and eggs were other good sources of protein for soldiers. Soldiers sometimes boiled eggs. They carried hard-boiled eggs in their pockets to eat during marches.

protein—proteins are things that are necessary for life. Proteins are found in cells, which are the tiny building blocks that make up all plants and animals

IRISH STEW

INGREDIENTS

2 tablespoons vegetable oil
1 boneless beef chuck roast
    (3 to 4 pounds)
1 pound whole new potatoes
1 pound carrots, peeled and cut
    into 1/2-inch (12-mm) pieces
1 tablespoon salt
1 teaspoon pepper
water

EQUIPMENT

measuring spoons
Dutch oven or large saucepan with lid
liquid measuring cup
fork

Ask an adult to help you prepare this recipe.

1. Pour 2 tablespoons vegetable oil in Dutch oven or saucepan, warm over medium heat.

2. Add beef chuck roast. Cook just until meat is brown on all sides.

3. Add potatoes, carrots, 1 tablespoon salt, and 1 teaspoon pepper.

4. Cover with 8 cups water. Bring to a boil over medium-high heat. Reduce heat to medium. Cook 2 to 2-1/2 hours or until meat is tender and easy to cut.

5. Place meat on platter.

6. Remove two potatoes with fork. Mash these potatoes with fork and stir mashed potatoes into the stew mixture to thicken the gravy.

Makes 6-8 servings.

CHAPTER 5

BREADS AND SOUPS

Union soldiers received rations to make their own bread. Instead of baking ovens, soldiers carried a cast iron pan with a lid and three short legs. This pan was called a **spider.** Soldiers could make biscuits and pancakes in a spider. Union soldiers also cooked **johnnycake** in spiders. Soldiers needed few ingredients and very little skill to cook this type of cornbread.

Hardtack is most often associated with the Civil War. This hard, thick cracker was made with flour, water, and salt. It was made extremely hard on purpose. It did not break up into crumbs. Hardtack was lightweight and easy to carry. It lasted a long time without spoiling. But it often had worms living in the holes and cracks. For this reason soldiers gave hardtack the name "worm castle." When their stomachs were empty and there was nothing else on hand, soldiers ate the wormy hardtack anyway.

spider—an iron skillet with three legs
johnnycake—a bread made with cornmeal, flour, eggs, and milk

JOHNNYCAKE

INGREDIENTS

1 cup water
1-1/2 cups ground yellow cornmeal
1/2 teaspoon salt
1/2 cup milk
2 tablespoons butter
molasses or syrup and
    butter for serving

EQUIPMENT

small saucepan
liquid measuring cup
large mixing bowl
dry-ingredient measuring cups
measuring spoons
wooden spoon
large skillet
spatula

Ask an adult to help you prepare this recipe.

1. Bring 1 cup water to boil in saucepan.

2. Combine 1-1/2 cups cornmeal, 1/2 teaspoon salt, 1 cup boiled water, and 1/2 cup milk in bowl. Stir well.

3. Melt 2 tablespoons butter in skillet over medium heat.

4. Pour 1 tablespoon of batter into skillet. Cook over medium heat 4 to 5 minutes on each side. Cook until edges are lacy and lightly browned. Turn gently with spatula.

5. Serve hot with molasses or maple syrup and butter.

Makes about 15 johnnycakes.

NAVY BEAN SOUP

Union soldiers cooked beans many ways. In the evenings soldiers sometimes dug a little hole and built a fire in it. They covered their pot of beans, put it in the hole, and let the beans cook through the night. Soldiers also added beans to soup. Yankees seasoned their soup with salt pork. The salt pork made the beans tastier and helped to fill the soldiers' stomachs. Any available fresh or dried vegetables or greens also went into the soup.

INGREDIENTS

1 cup (8 ounces) dried navy beans
5 cups water
1/2 pound salt pork
1 large onion (3/4 cup chopped)
2 large carrots (1 cup chopped)
1 large potato, unpeeled, cut into
    1/2-inch (12-mm) pieces
1 teaspoon salt
1/2 teaspoon pepper

EQUIPMENT

colander
Dutch oven or large saucepan
    with lid
liquid measuring cup
cutting board
sharp knife
vegetable peeler
measuring and wooden spoons
fork

Ask an adult to help you prepare this recipe.

1. Wash beans in colander. Discard any discolored beans.
2. Place beans in Dutch oven or saucepan. Cover with water 2 inches (5 cm) above beans. Soak beans overnight.
3. Drain beans in colander. Return beans to Dutch oven or saucepan. Add 5 cups water.
4. Cut criss-cross pattern into salt pork with fork. Add salt pork to beans.
5. Remove skin from onion. Chop onion. Peel 2 carrots with vegetable peeler. Chop carrots.
6. Stir in chopped onions and chopped carrots.
7. Bring to a boil. Cover, reduce heat, and simmer 45 minutes or until beans are tender.
8. Cut potato into 1/2-inch (12-mm) pieces. Add potato pieces, 1 teaspoon salt, and 1/2 teaspoon pepper. (Ask an adult for help with this step.)
9. Bring to a boil. Cover. Cook 15 minutes or until potato pieces are tender. If you are able to easily stick a fork through a potato without it falling apart, the potato is tender.

Makes 6-8 servings.

CHAPTER 6

DRIED AND FRESH FRUITS

Forests and farms provided fresh fruits for soldiers in the summer and autumn months. Union soldiers often picked wild berries during the summer. Union soldiers in the South paid for or helped themselves to peaches, watermelons, and other fruits from nearby farms and gardens. Apples were plentiful from August through October in many areas.

Fresh fruit was seldom available in the winter. Soldiers often ate dried apples. In the fall soldiers cut fresh apples into thin slices and let them dry in the sun. Sun-dried apples did not spoil or become rotten. In winter, soldiers soaked dried apples in water. They then fried the apples and spooned them into a pie crust to make a sweet dessert.

Dried apples provided vitamin C to the soldiers. Vitamin C prevented **scurvy**, a disease that makes the gums around a person's teeth bleed. Army hospitals sometimes distributed dried apples to the soldiers to keep them healthy.

scurvy—a disease from not getting enough vitamin C

SKILLET-FRIED APPLES

INGREDIENTS

5 Granny Smith or other cooking
    apples, unpeeled
4 tablespoons butter
1/2 cup brown sugar
1/2 teaspoon nutmeg

EQUIPMENT

cutting board
sharp knife
large skillet with lid
wooden spoon
dry-ingredient measuring cups
measuring spoons

Ask an adult to help you prepare this recipe.

1. Wash apples. Remove the core and
   seeds, but do not peel. Cut apples
   into 16 narrow wedges.
2. In skillet, melt butter over
   medium heat.
3. Add apples. Cover. Cook 5 minutes.
4. Add 4 tablespoons brown sugar
   and 1/2 teaspoon nutmeg. Stir well.
5. Cook covered 10 to 12 minutes or
   until apples are tender. Check apples

every few minutes during cooking. Add extra butter if needed to
keep apples from sticking to pan. If you are able to easily stick a
fork through an apple without it falling apart, the apple is tender.

Makes 6 to 8 servings.

CHAPTER 7

LIFE BACK HOME

Life in the North did not change much for those who were rich before the Civil War began. Wealthy people made even more money by selling food, clothing, and weapons to the Union Army.

Life changed more for Northerners who did not have much money. Wages for workers decreased during the war years. But the cost of food and living expenses increased. Food prices rose as much as 75 percent during the Civil War. Union families could not afford to buy many food items during the war. Like Union soldiers, citizens often went hungry.

Women took over much of the hard labor when the men in their families left to become soldiers. Young boys hauled livestock to slaughterhouses so soldiers would have meat. Boys sawed firewood for their mothers, their neighbors, and sometimes even for soldiers at nearby camps. They took care of the animals and crops. Girls helped by taking care of younger children. They knitted socks for the soldiers, helped tend gardens, and cooked.

MACARONI AND CHEESE

INGREDIENTS

8 ounces macaroni
2 tablespoons butter for greasing
3 eggs
2 cups milk
3-1/2 cups shredded cheddar cheese
1 teaspoon salt
1/4 teaspoon pepper

EQUIPMENT

large saucepan
colander
2-quart baking dish
mixing bowl
fork
liquid measuring cup
measuring and wooden spoons
aluminum foil
paper towel or napkin

Ask an adult to help you prepare this recipe.

1. Cook macaroni according to package directions, omitting salt. Drain in colander.

2. Heat oven to 400°F (200°C). Use paper towel or napkin to grease baking dish with butter.

3. Put macaroni in baking dish.

4. In bowl, beat 3 eggs with a fork. Add 2 cups milk, 2-1/2 cups cheese, 1 teaspoon salt, and 1/4 teaspoon pepper. Pour over macaroni. Stir to combine mixture with macaroni.

5. Cover with foil. Bake at 400°F (200°C) for 40 minutes. Uncover. Sprinkle with remaining 1 cup cheese. Bake 5 minutes or until cheese melts.

Makes 8 servings.

CHAPTER 8

THE UNION AT CHRISTMAS

Christmas was the most widely celebrated holiday for Civil War troops. Families and friends of the soldiers sent packages from home. The food they received was good, but just being remembered was more important for most homesick soldiers.

Christmas festivities back home were usually scarce. Wives and children had to make do with less money. Soldiers were not always paid regularly, and couldn't always send it home. With fewer men to do the chores at home, families did not have as much time for celebrating. Most families and communities attended church services together on Christmas Day.

TEA CAKE COOKIES

INGREDIENTS

1 tablespoon butter for greasing
5 cups all-purpose flour
1 teaspoon baking soda
1/2 teaspoon ground nutmeg
1 cup (2 sticks) butter
1 cup buttermilk (or 1 cup milk
    plus 1 tablespoon vinegar)
2 large eggs
2 cups sugar
additional flour, if needed

EQUIPMENT

baking sheet
large mixing bowl
dry-ingredient measuring cups
measuring spoons
fork or pastry blender
medium mixing bowl
liquid measuring cup
wooden spoon
pot holders
paper towel or napkin

Ask an adult to help you prepare this recipe.

1. Heat oven to 375°F (190°C). Use paper towel or napkin to
   grease baking sheet with butter.

2. Combine 5 cups flour, 1 teaspoon baking soda, and 1/2 teaspoon nutmeg
   in large bowl. Cut in 2 sticks butter with fork or pastry blender until
   mixture looks like coarse crumbs. (Ask an adult to help you with this step.)

3. In medium bowl, stir together 1 cup milk, 2 eggs, and 2 cups sugar. Pour
   into dry ingredients. Stir well. Wash hands, then lightly coat fingertips with
   butter. Shape dough into 1-inch (2.5-cm) balls. (If mixture is too wet to roll,
   add 1/2 cup additional flour and try again.) Place balls on baking sheets.

4. Dip fork in flour, then use it to flatten balls. Bake 10 to 12 minutes
   or until golden brown.

Makes 5 dozen cookies.

Union families celebrated Christmas with special meals. New Englanders ate roast turkey with stuffing. Near the coast, family Christmas menus featured crab and other seafood. Cooks made stuffing with fresh oysters. In the Midwest, families ate pork chops or ham for Christmas dinner. Winter vegetables such as potatoes, turnips, parsnips, and rutabagas were often served as side dishes. Cooks used cranberries and dried fruits in sauces and desserts.

Special cakes and candies were an important part of Christmas celebrations during the Civil War. After the first year of the Civil War, sugar and butter became scarce. Northern families saved these ingredients to bake cookies, gingerbread, and other treats for special occasions such as Christmas.

GINGERBREAD

INGREDIENTS

1 tablespoon butter
   or margarine
2-1/2 cups all-purpose flour
1-1/2 teaspoons baking soda
1/2 cup (1 stick) butter, softened
1-1/4 cups molasses
1 egg
1-1/2 teaspoons cinnamon
1-1/2 teaspoons allspice
1 cup very hot water

EQUIPMENT

9-inch by 9-inch (23-cm by
   23-cm) baking pan
large bowl
dry-ingredient measuring cups
measuring spoons
wooden spoon
fork
liquid measuring cup
wooden toothpick
pot holders
paper towel or napkin

Ask an adult to help you prepare this recipe.

1. Preheat oven to 350°F (180°C). Use paper towel or napkin
   to grease baking pan with butter.

2. In large bowl, combine flour and baking soda. Cut soft butter
   into flour mixture with fork.

3. Add molasses, egg, cinnamon, allspice, and water. Stir well.

4. Pour batter into baking pan. Bake 35 to 40 minutes, or until
   wooden toothpick inserted near the center comes out clean.
   (Ask an adult to help you with this step.)

Makes 9 servings.

GLOSSARY

barracks (BAR-uhks)–the part of a fort where soldiers sleep

buttermilk (BUHT·ur·milk)–the liquid left after butter has been churned from milk or cream

canteen (kan-TEEN)–a small metal container for holding water

cornmeal (KORN-meel)–corn that is coarsely ground

Dutch oven (DUHCH-UHV-uhn)–a large covered pot

forage (FOR-ij)–to search for food

johnnycake (JOHN-ee-kake)–a bread made with cornmeal, flour, eggs, and milk

persimmon (pur-SIM-uhn)–an orange-red fruit that is shaped like a plum and is sweet and soft when ripe

plantation (plan-TAY-shuhn)–large farm found in warm areas; before the Civil War, plantations in the South used slave labor

protein (PROH-teen)–proteins are things that are necessary for life. Proteins are found in cells, which are the tiny building blocks that make up all plants and animals

ration (RASH-uhn)–a soldier's daily share of food

route (ROUT)–the road or course followed to get somewhere

scurvy (SCURV-ee)–a disease from not getting enough vitamin C

secede (si-SEED)–to formally withdraw from a group or an organization, often to form another organization

spider (SPYE-dur)–an iron skillet with three legs

surrender (suh-REN-dur)–to give up, or admit defeat in a fight or battle

READ MORE

Ford, Carin T. *An Overview of the American Civil War Through Primary Sources.* The Civil War Through Primary Sources. Berkeley Heights, N.J.: Enslow, 2013.

Howell, Sara. *The Civil War: Frontier Soldiers and Their Families.* Frontline Families. New York: Gareth Stevens Publishing, 2016.

Hurt, Douglas R. *Food and Agriculture during the Civil War.* Santa Barbara, Calif.: Praeger, 2016.

INTERNET SITES

FactHound offers a safe, fun way to find Internet sites related to this book. All of the sites on FactHound have been researched by our staff.

Here's all you do:

Visit *www.facthound.com*

Type in this code: 9781515723530

Super-cool stuff! Check out projects, games and lots more at **www.capstonekids.com**

INDEX

Civil War, 8, 9, 18, 24, 28
Confederate States of America, 7
cooking, 11, 18, 20, 24

desserts, 14, 22, 28
disease, 22

families, 24, 26, 28
Fort Sumter, 8
fruits, 12, 14, 22, 28

government, 7

hardtack, 18
holidays, 26, 28
hospitals, 22

Lincoln, Abraham, 7, 8

meat, 16, 24, 28
messes, 11

plantations, 6
protein, 16

rations, 12, 13, 16, 18
Rebels, 8, 10
Republican Party, 7

slavery, 6, 7, 8
South Carolina, 7, 8
starvation, 8
supply wagons, 10, 16

vegetables, 20, 28

wages, 24, 26
water, 9, 18, 22

Yankees, 8, 10, 20